And…… are alpacas REALLY scary?!

By

Joanne Louise Dell

Illustrated by

Kristian Hewitt

And...... are alpacas REALLY scary?!

Copyright © 2016 Joanne Louise Dell. All rights reserved.
First paperback edition printed 2016 in the United Kingdom

A catalogue record for this book is available from the British Library.

ISBN 978-0-9935048-0-8

No part of this book shall be reproduced or transmitted in any form or by any means, electronic or mechanical, including photocopying, recording, or by any information retrieval system without written permission of the publisher.

Published by Abbotts View Publishing
For more copies of this book, please email: Jo.dell@abbottsviewalpacas.co.uk
Tel: 07989 063595

Printed in Great Britain

Acknowledgement: I would like to thank my family for their encouragement and support, the animals who have taught me so much and each and every visitor who has come to share our farm, especially the children who arrive scared and leave with a smile on their faces. You were my inspiration for this story. And, alpacas aren't REALLY scary :0)

Although every precaution has been taken in the preparation of this book, the publisher and author assume no responsibility for errors or omissions. Neither is any liability assumed for damages resulting from the use of this information contained herein.

"We're going to see **alpacas**"
My mummy said to me
"Are you sure? Do we have to?
Will we be home for tea?"

I'm a bit scared of animals
And **alpacas**! What are they?
Are they small or are they BIG?
Do they fight? Do they play?

Are they scary? Are they friendly?
Are they happy or are they sad?
Are they small and cute and cuddly
Or big and strong, like my dad?

Do they have lots of teeth?
Do they bite? Can they roar?
Have they ever eaten adults
Or little children before?

Oh now I'm really worried!
I'm not sure about this at all!
"Can't we go to the park instead
And play with my new ball??!"

My mummy smiles and cuddles me
"Don't worry, it'll be okay
I'm sure **alpacas** are lovely
And they're not very far away."

So we climb into the car
And I bring Teddy to keep me safe

If she's with me then I am brave
I WILL be brave at this new place!

I'm clutching Teddy tightly
As we climb out of the car
I can see some animals in the fields
They're not too close, quite far.

The farmer looks quite friendly
She smiles and says "Hello."

She gets down so she's as small as me
And says "Hi Teddy, my name's Jo."

"So you've come to meet our **alpacas**?
Have you met any before?"
I clutch Teddy really tightly
Shake my head and look at the floor.

"Well they'll be very pleased to meet you two,
They're really nosy you see,
And whenever there are visitors
They know there will be treats."

I screw my eyes up tightly as
My heart begins to pound
What if Ted and me
are their treat to eat?
I sit down on the ground.

I think this is a bad idea!
I really want to go!!
I look up at mum who smiles and says
"There's food to feed them, you know!"

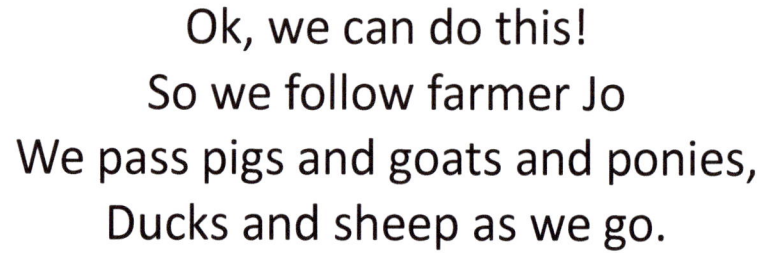

Ok, we can do this!
So we follow farmer Jo
We pass pigs and goats and ponies,
Ducks and sheep as we go.

"So here are the girl **alpacas**
With their babies, aren't they sweet?
Would you like to hold a feeding tray
And give them all a treat?"

Ok so they aren't really scary,
They're fluffy and quite tall.
They've long necks and huge eyes
And their babies are quite small.

"Come close and meet the little ones,
The babies are called cria
They've all been born this summer
Each mum only has one a year."

"These two are being bottle fed
Would you like to have a go?
You can help Ted hold a bottle
Here, try it" says farmer Jo.

So I help Teddy hold the bottle
The milk is goats milk, warm not hot.
"The little fawn one is called Dolly,
And that brown one – she's called Dot."

I'm feeding a baby **alpaca**!
I am – all on my own!
Well, Teddy's kind of helping
I can't wait to tell Daddy when I'm home!

Dot's eyes are huge and dark and shiny,
Her lashes are long and black.
Her nose is soft and her fur is too
I felt it on her back.

Jo says "**Alpacas** are unusual,
And are a bit scared of us.
They don't often let us stroke them.
They don't really like a fuss.

But if we're quiet and gentle,
They might let us stroke their necks
But never touch their top knots,
That's the fluffy bit on their head."

I've stroked a baby **alpaca**!
And I've given her a feed!
"When you're both a little older
You could come and walk her on a lead."

And I've fed a big **alpaca**!
I gave her treats from a tray
They all ran over when they saw the food
And then I got really brave….

I fed them from my hand!
Oh their noses are soft and sweet!
And did you know that they don't bite
Because they only have bottom teeth?

And farmer Jo told us that
It's nearly time to shear

That's when they cut their fluff off
And they do it once a year.

She took us to the cafe
And gave us some fluff to keep,
She let us feel how soft it is
And we also felt some sheep.

I think I love **alpacas**
And so does Teddy too
So mummy bought us one to keep;
I think I'll call her Sue.

I can't wait to tell my friends
That **alpacas** aren't REALLY scary.
They're cute and soft with the biggest eyes
And ears that are all hairy.

And I'll show Daddy how to feed them
From a bottle and from your hand

And I'll tell him that if he wants to meet them,
Well, he really can!

Fascinating Alpaca Facts

- Alpacas originate from the Altiplano in west-central South America, bordering Peru, Chile & Bolivia.

- Alpacas are camelids, related to llamas and camels.

- Alpacas have a lifespan of 15-20 years.

- Alpacas stand at about 1 metre tall at the withers. An adult female (Hembra) weighs about 65kg and a male (Macho) about 75kg.

- There are 2 types of alpaca: Huacaya (pronounced wa-ky-ya) and Suri. Huacayas need shearing once a year, Suris every two years.

- Alpacas are herd animals and only feel safe with their own kind. They are good fox guards, protecting sheep and poultry.

- Alpacas were developed primarily as a fleece producing animal, meat is secondary but is a low cholesterol lean red meat.

- Alpacas are induced ovulators so can be bred at anytime.

- Alpacas are pregnant for about 11.5 months. Their young are called cria and they rarely have twins. Cria weigh 6-8kg at birth.

- Alpacas are semi-ruminants and survive mainly on grass and hay. They have 3 stomach compartments.

- Alpacas can spit! But only when provoked or frightened.

- At the front of their mouths alpacas only have teeth at the bottom, with a hard pad at the top. They don't have hooves but have foot pads with two toenails.

- In the UK there are 22 recognised fleece colours, in the USA 16, Australia 12 but in Peru over 52!

- Alpacas can be halter trained and are very inquisitive so enjoy being taken for a walk, but prefer a friend to come along too. They love to explore new things and people, but don't appreciate being stroked!

- DNA testing in 2001 revealed that alpacas descended from the vicuña and not the llama/guanaco as was previously thought.

www.ingramcontent.com/pod-product-compliance
Lightning Source LLC
Chambersburg PA
CBHW041126300426
44113CB00002B/80